Whole Earth Meditation

Text and Photographs by

Joan Sauro, C.S.J.

San Diego, California

LuraMedia ™

Printed on recycled paper with soy-based inks.

© 1986, 1992 Joan Sauro, C.S.J.
International Copyright Secured
Publisher's Catalog Number LM-633
Printed and bound in the United States of America

Cover image by Sara Steele. "Desertscape/Near Abiquiu."
  © 1985 by Sara Steele. All Rights Reserved.
Cover design by Bernadette G. Littlefield.
Book design by Linda Lockowitz, San Diego, California.
Photographs by Joan Sauro, C.S.J.

LuraMedia
7060 Miramar Road, Suite 104
San Diego, California 92121

Library of Congress Cataloging-in-Publication Data
Sauro, Joan.
      Whole earth meditation : ecology for the spirit / text and
    photographs by Joan Sauro.
        p.   cm.
      ISBN 0-931055-89-X
      1. Meditations.   I. Title.
    BX2182.2.S333   1992
    242—dc20
                                                          91-45190
                                                              CIP

Joan Sauro, a member of the Sisters of St. Joseph of Carondelet, lives in Syracuse, New York, where she keeps a small garden. Joan is the recipient of a Caps grant for fiction from the New York State Council on the Arts and a fellowship for fiction from the New York Foundation for the Arts. Her short story, "Death in the Convent," published in COMMONWEAL, was judged Best Short Story for 1989 by the Catholic Press Association.

for my father and mother,
Anthony and Helen

CONTENTS

Some of these pieces originally appeared in *America*, *Sisters Today*, and *Weavings*. The author is grateful to the respective editors.

PREFACE

This book is a story about us. The photographs are all taken from a family album — mother and father, brothers, sisters, aunts, uncles, and cousins to the nth degree. This is a family reunion where you can get to know the relatives better.

In another sense, this is a book of self-portraits, taken from different angles, in different lighting and seasons. Another kind of reunion wherein you may become better acquainted with yourself.

A book is to be talked to. If you like, talk back in the white space. Or leave it fallow and see what grows.

When you close the book, maybe you will go to the nearest window and bless the publisher, editors, and author, all of whom are at their windows blessing you.

BEGINNING THE JOURNEY

♦ ♦ ♦

OUTER TO INNER

ONCE UPON A TIME IN MY LIFE I HAD TWO HOMES. ONE WAS IN ALBANY, WHERE I LIVED AND WORKED. THE OTHER WAS IN SYRACUSE, WHERE I WAS BORN AND WHERE MY FAMILY STILL LIVED. THE TWO HOMES WERE CONNECTED BY THE GREYHOUND BUS LINE, WHICH I RODE AT HOLIDAYS, BIRTHDAYS, AND SUMMER VACATIONS.

MIDPOINT ON THE JOURNEY BETWEEN THE TWO HOMES, NEAR LITTLE FALLS, THE EARTH HAD BEEN DEEPLY CUT AND A WEDGE REMOVED IN ORDER TO BUILD THE ROAD THE BUS TRAVELED. JUST BEYOND OUR WINDOWS STEEP ROCKS AND CLIFFS ROSE HIGH ON EITHER SIDE.

A HUSH ALWAYS CAME OVER THE PEOPLE IN THE BUS WHENEVER WE PASSED THROUGH THAT STRETCH OF TOWERING HILLS. THERE, TO LEFT AND RIGHT, WAS A CROSS SECTION OF EARTH, STANDING FOR MILES WITH ALL OF ITS INNER LAYERS EXPOSED.

How vast and intricate it was, how infinite the number of nooks and crannies. Here the land jutted and fretted; there it slid, folded in upon itself, and burgeoned in spite of the odds. Who could see it all, let alone come to know and understand?

Unconsciously, my eye followed the twists and turns, the sculptured folds and faults, and soon I was lost in them. God must transform this terrain, I thought. God must transform it inch by inch, with fire if need be.

By this time I was no longer looking at the outer, natural earth. I was looking at my own inner world, similarly cut away in a cross section. And I was asking God to transform me.

SILENTLY AND SIMPLY I PASSED FROM PLACE TO PLACE, AS IF VIEWING MY INNER LANDSCAPE FOR THE FIRST TIME. ALL THE WHILE THE BUS WAS GOING FAR AND WIDE, I WAS GOING DEEP AND DEEPER.

THROUGH BRUSH AND BRIAR I WENT, OVER ROCKY LEDGE, DOWN DARK RAVINE, AND INTO THE REGION OF FIRE AND ICE. IT WAS PASSAGE WITHOUT WORDS, WITHOUT COMPASS OR MAP.

SOME OF THE LAYERS I SAW WERE FAMILIAR. MANY I DID NOT RECOGNIZE AS MY OWN.

SOME I STILL DO NOT RECOGNIZE,

ALTHOUGH I HAVE TAKEN THAT

JOURNEY MANY TIMES SINCE.

BUT I AM LEARNING AS I GO.

A curled and dried up leaf, the size of a thumbnail, falls what seems an infinite space from tree to rock below. There it rests, leaf on rock, two dead things, and what is that to me? Why should I sit spellbound, drag a lawn chair up and down the yard as leaves fall, grass blades twitch? What's to be said of one who loves leaf on rock, who in winter sits in front of windows looking out, this time dragging a chair from window to window as the light moves. Is this the way to redeem the earth? There are people starving in Ethiopia, as I well know. Shooting each other in Ireland, El Salvador, Chicago. Hanging by their fingernails on the very street where I live.

Put another way: Why make the journey to the interior when there's all this to be done in the world?

One day I was out with everyone else on the block raking up the fallen leaves, admiring their colored handprints on grass and pavement. Up above, clumps of leaves still clung to trees, tossing and turning like restless sleepers. The sound of them was of an ocean tossing, and I imagined endless blue waters. As I looked, rake in hand, I felt a hook in my lower jaw and that great Fisher of souls out in the deep in hip boots reeling me in on a line sharper than a razor's edge.

I fought back, like the fish in Elizabeth Bishop's poem, tossing and leaping in a white spray. When the line was slack, I circled blue pools, explored muddy waters, bit whatever bright thing dangled before me. When the line grew taut, I fought tooth and nail. Finally, like the fish, I was hauled dripping into the boat, my eye gleaming, other hooks and bits of broken line hanging like trophies from my jaw.

But there is no breaking that line sharper than a razor's edge. All of the saints knew this because they tried, some of them fiercely.

In the rafters of my father's garage, in among the barrels and boards, there is an old picture of one of my favorites. There, in a marvelous gilt-edge frame, five feet by two, Theresa, called the Little Flower, gazes straight out of an enclosed garden lush with flowers. This is the woman who never traveled beyond the garden walls. She, too, was enamored of leaves and twitching grass, people in distant lands and journeys to the interior. In the picture she cradles a cross and a blanket of red roses. Theresa gazed out of the garden of my bedroom wall the whole of my growing up life.

The other day I asked my mother where she ever got such a picture. She smiled and said a traveling salesman was passing by the house when we were small and she bought it from him. But why this particular picture, I asked, of all the ones he had. She shrugged her shoulders and in her inscrutable logic said, "I like roses!"

Out of such logic grew my passion for windows. For whatever Theresa meant to do with her life, she has come to mean for me the blessing of the earth seen lovingly through windows, the unbinding of chains on people you do not see through love sent in their direction.

If Theresa in her garden enclosed could do this, so can I.

Up in the rafters of the garage Theresa smiles like Mona Lisa. Write this: She loved this earth, was wild with joy over a leaf falling on rock and resting there, knew in her joy that Someone in hip boots was out there noticing, too. And not only leaves.

She knew she was caught — hook, line, and sinker.

WALKING YOUR INNER EARTH

◆ ◆ ◆

LAYER UPON LAYER

THE DAY I FIRST SAW INNER EARTH FROM A BUS WINDOW, I WAS ONE OF MANY TRAVELERS POISED BETWEEN HOMES. WE SAT ARM TO ARM, SKIN TO SKIN. FOR A LITTLE WHILE WE WERE ALL ANYONE ELSE HAD, HOMELESS. AT EVERY ABRUPT TURN THE BUS MADE, WE WERE THROWN HELTER SKELTER INTO ONE ANOTHER, WHILE OUTSIDE OF OUR WINDOWS THE VAST OUTER WORLD WAS SHOWING US WHAT OUR INNER EARTH LOOKED LIKE.

AND SO IT IS WITH YOU. YOU, TOO, ARE A TRAVELER THROUGH THIS EARTH, SHARING WITH EVERYONE ELSE NOT ONLY AN OUTER WORLD THAT NEEDS YOUR CARE, BUT ALSO A PRECIOUS INNER EARTH THAT IS ITS REFLECTION. YOU HAVE ONLY TO LOOK TO THIS INNER EARTH OF YOURS, GENTLY, AND WITHOUT HASTE, TO DISCOVER HOW REMARKABLY SIMILAR TO THE OUTER NATURAL EARTH YOU ARE. SHE IS A CLOSE RELATIVE OF YOURS.

LIKE HER, YOU ARE LAYER UPON LAYER, LAID OVER AND UNDER, THICK AND THIN, EVEN AND IRREGULAR. YOU ARE STURDY IN SOME PLACES, CRUMBLING IN OTHERS. AT REST. AND RESTLESS.

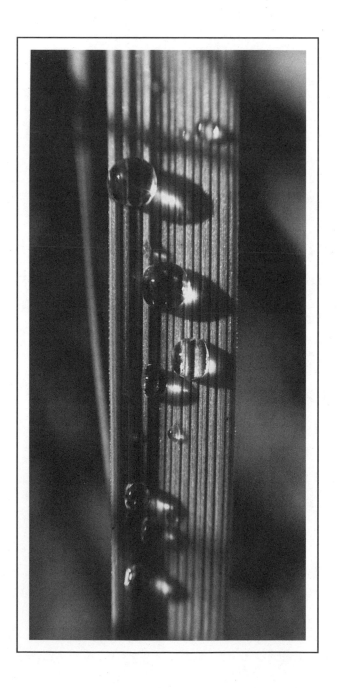

IN SOME LAYERS YOU ARE SOAKED
WITH WATER, GREEN WITH LIFE,
AND NURTURING.

IN OTHER LAYERS YOU ARE HARD,
LIKE MARBLE, SLATE, A ROLLING
AVALANCHE.

YOU CAN STAND IN PARCHED DESERT
PLACES INSIDE YOURSELF.

AND YOU CAN STAND BEFORE
PLACES THAT ARE UNREACHABLE,
UNKNOWN TO YOU. DEEP WITHIN
THERE ARE LANDS WHERE EVEN YOU
HAVE NEVER BEEN.

IN SOME LAYERS YOUR EARTH
STRETCHES OUT TO CATCH THE SUN.
HOW WARM AND VERY BEAUTIFUL
YOU ARE THERE.

IN OTHER PLACES YOU ARE FILLED WITH DEEP CREVICES AND HOLES WHERE NO SUN REACHES. NEITHER DOES ANY OTHER PERSON REACH YOU THERE.

IN YOUR INNER SELF THERE ARE LAYERS OF COLLAPSE WHERE VIOLENT UPHEAVALS HAVE GONE ON, LEAVING YOU WEAK, UNRESTORED, AND VULNERABLE.

This is your inner earth, its slopes and plateaus, its reds, greens, pinks, deep down browns and grays. You are jagged and smooth to touch, filled with light and shadow, heaps and hollows.

Take off your shoes. The place where you are standing is holy.

When the glacial ice receded, it left behind the corrugated face of Watkins Glen, a vast and complicated gorge, at once lovely and dangerous. Some passageways are so narrow that the impinging earth threatens to swallow the climber. Currents drop gracefully, at first, then churn and power down twisted chutes to scour the rock into big bellied pots.

I touch the earth sandpaper smooth, burnished mahogany. I touch layers of sandstone weaving through shale beds and am myself touched with mist and flying foam. I photograph every layer in view, so that I will remember the grace and energy that pulses in the earth, in the layers of my own heart.

Then I see the two of them up ahead, passing behind the Rainbow Falls. She is in one of those ubiquitous pantsuits that render a woman shapeless. He is in clean shirt and dark blue pants, shiny in back. They wear good and respectable clothes, as people on an outing do. Middle America on the edge of retirement, out for a breath of fresh air, climbing the Glen together on a bright blue autumn day.

On the man's feet are his best shoes, not yet a month old, judging from the looks. The brown leather and thick cushion soles are still clean. But already the back of the man's right shoe is wrinkled like an accordion from where his heel pronates. With each step the man takes up the canyon, his foot rolls inward. He is slowly caving in, but he keeps on, a gentle hand on her waist as they pass behind the gauzy bridal veil.

On the day the two of them walked up the aisle in brand new clothes into a brand new life he pronated. On that bright day he never gave it a thought. He doesn't give it a thought today either, though his feet hurt, and he worries in the slow caving in whether the money from his middle America job will hold out, whether he will be able to take care of her to the end, and beyond, should she outlive him, and numbers show she well may.

Today I shoot ninety-six breathtaking slides of Watkins Glen, but all I can remember is a man's broken, accordion shoe.

Her nun's undersleeves were made of black silky material, gauzy looking, and sheer. She was our music teacher when I was a beginner in the religious life, but the thing I remember most is not the music but her undersleeves. Down the center she had ironed a crease that could cut cake, and that crease was all I could look at when she directed our singing voices. It was all I dared look at, for a direct look into her chiseled face was against the rule.

The crease in her nun's veil was as sharp as the crease in her undersleeves and rose over her white band and forehead like a church steeple. No matter what day of the week it was, Sister Margaret seemed always to be wearing Sunday clothes.

But it is that graceful right hand coming out of the gauzy black sleeve with the crease that I remember most. My contralto was clear, always on key, but it reached new glories under her direction. I could sing any hymn, reach any note, however high or low, so long as that hand waved over me.

And so I loved Saturday morning classes in the music room. Even more I loved Friday night rehearsal in the dim choir loft where a small, select band sang like angels. High up in the choir loft we stood in the shadows and sang in three powerful streams which Sister Margaret took in her nimble fingers and wove into one mighty river.

One morning at the Saturday classes she herself sang. It was the *Ave Maria*, sung in the purest voice I had ever heard in my life. It was sharper, more cutting in its intensity than the crease in her sleeve. Suddenly the room where we were sitting grew unaccountably small and brittle.

Fifteen years later Sister Margaret left the convent. She fought with herself for years and thought she had reached a definite, peaceful decision to stay. Then one morning she left. "I just put on my shoes and they no longer fit," was all she said.

I thought it frightening, that you could be wearing the same good, trusted shoes every day of your life and then one day realize they did not fit. I wanted to ask her how it had happened. Did her feet suddenly grow in the night? Was it that the shoes had never fit? Had they been crippling her all that time, even as she sang? Did they break down like an old accordion and become unfit to walk the earth? Or was it the earth itself, once so nurturing, that turned into a rolling avalanche?

I would like to have Sister Margaret's shoes, for grateful remembrance. I would bronze them, her black shoes and the man's wrinkled ones.

DISCOVERING YOUR DEEPEST SELF

◆ ◆ ◆

HISTORY AND DREAMS

ALL OF YOUR HISTORY IS WRITTEN ON THE WALLS INSIDE YOU: YOUR PARENTS, FAMILY, UPBRINGING AND EDUCATION, THE HOMES YOU LIVED IN, THE PLACES YOU VISITED, EVERY BOOK YOU EVER READ, EVERY SONG YOU EVER SANG, EVERY PERSON YOU EVER LOVED AND WHO LOVED YOU. THEY ARE ALL PRESENT INSIDE YOU.

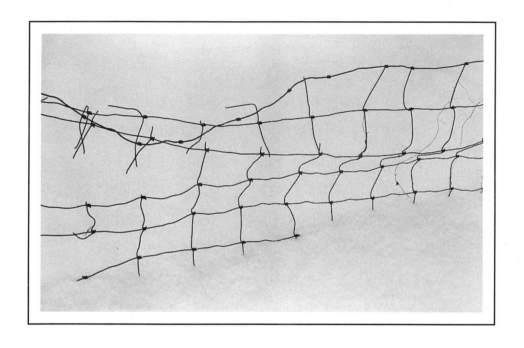

So is every person you ever disliked or ignored, and who hated you. Each of them is also present within you.

ALL OF YOUR DREAMS AND
LONGINGS ARE REFLECTED HERE,
YOUR REMARKABLE INNER LIGHT.

ALL OF YOUR FAULTS AND BREAKS
ARE HERE, TOO, UPHEAVALS OF
EARTH, PLACES WHERE YOU HAVE
BEEN HURT AND ARE LIKELY TO BE
HURT AGAIN.

THE MORE YOU WALK YOUR INNER PATH, THE MORE YOU TOUCH YOUR DEEPEST SELF, THE MORE YOU WILL FIND THAT GOD HAS BEEN THERE BEFORE YOU, WRITING IN EVERY LAYER THE NAME ONLY YOU CAN READ.

GOD LIVES IN THE WIDE SWEEP OF YOUR INNER GEOGRAPHY AND IN THE SMALLEST MOLECULE OF YOUR HISTORY. IT IS TIME TO COME HOME.

All of my great aunts were called "zia," which is Italian for "aunt." Two in particular I remember — Zia Mary Giuseppe and Zia Angie. They were sisters. Zia Mary Giuseppe was short, wore her hair in a bun, and had strong arms for making the pasta. Zia Angie was tall, with the same strong arms, same bun in the back of her head.

Zia Angie and Uncle Patsy were childless, which seemed unusual to me, and lived in a house that was always dark. That house is only a block away from where I live now, and so I often pass by. Sometimes I try to look through the fancy bay window the new owners cut into the front room of the house.

Behind that window there used to be a dark parlor where late Sunday afternoons we children sat with our father and Uncle Patsy, listening to the old Philco and the mysteries of Nick Carter, private detective. He was followed by chilling tales that ended with a frightening warning: "Who knows what evil lurks in the heart of man. The Shadow knows!" The voice laughed, a kind of gaggle far back in the throat, as darkness slipped over the window sill and down the walls over to the radio.

I suppose our mother and Zia Angie were in the kitchen talking around the brown porcelain table. Strange things came out of the kitchen, too — like tasteless, white cookies, and the rabbits Uncle Patsy shot, cooked into a strong, wild stew and spooned onto our plates.

But the parlor was my favorite, with the children sitting like soldiers in the stiff dark chairs, the men with cigars and small glasses of wine, and "The Shadow." I always sat near the only light there was, next to Zia Angie's best lamp. It had a hundred pencil-thin crystals hanging around the rim like transparent icicles. I watched for unguarded moments to slide a finger along the bottoms and set in motion a host of tingling crystals, the play of a hundred thousand lights.

There was a certain mystery to that home, and a great sense of shelter and protection. Not a bad thing for a Sunday afternoon.

It is a long time since, and the old aunt and uncle are long gone. Their house was broken up and the various pieces sold to the highest bidders. My sister Pat salvaged an old wash basin and a few ancient gardening tools. No one knows who has the box with "The Shadow" in it, or the light of a hundred dangling crystals.

Every time I walk through that layer of my childhood, I have a pervading sense of a warm, sheltering God. Then I did not know what name to call God. I knew only what a child could know, and that was a good home to be together in when the lights went down on holy Sunday.

SAVORING EVERY SEASON

◆ ◆ ◆

STRUGGLE AND JOY

GOD IS IN THE CLEAR WATER THAT RUSHES OVER YOU, SOAKING EVERY LAYER, AND WASHING. GOD SURPRISES YOU IN HIDDEN SPRINGS THAT YOU NEVER IMAGINED WERE THERE.

GOD IS ALSO IN EVERY DRIED UP,
LIFELESS PLACE INSIDE YOU. JUST
WHERE YOU DO NOT THINK TO LOOK.

GOD IS IN THE FIERCE WIND,
THE SEASON OF STRUGGLE.
THE TIME OF LOSS.

AND GOD IS IN JOYOUS TIMES
WHEN YOUR EARTH SPLITS ITS SEAMS,
AND LIFE, GOODNESS, FERTILITY
ABOUND.

IN EVERY SEASON OF YOUR LIFE,
GOD IS WITH YOU IN EVERY LAYER.

THERE IS A PEARL IN EVERY SEASON.

FIND IT. THEN GIVE ALL YOU HAVE

TO CLAIM IT.

The way our fathers leave us is in staggers. I don't mean just their bodies, my father's body, sinking down in the car seat, so that all I see in front of me is his brown wool dress cap and a white fringe of hair. There is a small curve of moon sinking below the top of the seat even as I look.

My father is shrinking like a piece of yard goods washed and dried too many times. He no longer fits expectations and is pulling in on himself, all the threads tightening.

By contrast, my Uncle Tim, who is next to my father and driving, fills the seat, his blue baseball cap barely clearing the car roof, his arms thick and capable in the white wool knit sweater. Some one of these miles we will lose my father, I just know it, in between talk of baseball and the weather. He will continue sinking and drop out of the bottom of the car and into the earth he loves.

My father used to be a prolific gardener, planting two hundred feet of vegetables to feed his wife and five children. Along one side of the garden, he dug two clay horseshoe pits. My father was also a championship horseshoe pitcher.

While other kids watched their dads roll up bowling scores at the local alley, I watched mine throw perfect ringers around iron stakes, heard them clang, slide and thud into thick, moist clay. Sometimes my father tied bundles of match sticks around the top of the stake and then, from forty feet away, threw ringers that struck the blue match heads. Small flames leaped like birthday candles around the stake, and we children screamed with delight over such fireworks.

This day of the sinking moon we reach the church parking lot before the sun rises and there, in the light of my Uncle

Tim's car beams, I help my father out of the car without seeming to, hand him his silver cane with the black rubber hand grip.

We have come to church this morning to celebrate my father's birthday with a Mass in honor of his parents. We have come mostly so that my father can hear his parents' names, *Joseph* and *Michelina*, proclaimed aloud in the church, alongside the statues of the holy ones, with the banks of candles flickering in red jars. Nice touch, I think, and tell my father he has an eye for timing. He reminds me that the day is also the anniversary of his mother's death. And so it is, she having laid down her life to give him birth, which is why each of his birthdays is a somber event.

Inside, we are joined by my father's aunt, lone remaining sister to the dead woman. It is a year since I have seen my great aunt and, to my horror, I see that the lower half of her face is vanishing. Lines in the face are one thing, but this is jaw and mouth disappearing.

She kisses me on the lips and says, "*Buon giorno.*"

I look over at my father with his hands folded, and I know what he is thinking. My father actually looks forward to the day when the mother he never knew comes for him. One Mother's Day he wrote her a letter to that effect and sent it to the local newspaper where it was so featured that people called my father all afternoon. I half expected one of the callers to be his mother, and I was glad when the day ended.

For I have no doubt that she will come for him. Only not just yet, I tell her from the church pew. Today's his birthday. Not just yet.

EXPERIENCING RENEWAL

◆ ◆ ◆

EMPTY TO FULL

Most of all, God is in the worn, embattled, broken-down layers because God has a long history of loving the poor and the weak. This is where to look for God most in yourself — where you are broken and vulnerable. Where you are scarred and need God's healing.

Look for God where your defense is weakest. At the break in the wall, the crack in the earth, the ground shifting out of control.

Go to the place called barren.
Stand in the place called empty.
And you will find god there.

THE SPIRIT OF GOD BREATHES EVERYWHERE WITHIN YOU, JUST AS IN THE BEGINNING, FILLING LIGHT PLACE AND DARK...GREEN EARTH AND DRY.

THUS DOES GOD RENEW THE FACE OF
THE EARTH. GOD ALWAYS BREAKS
THROUGH AT YOUR WEAKEST POINT,
WHERE YOU LEAST RESIST.

GOD'S LOVE GROWS, FULLNESS UPON

FULLNESS, WHERE YOU CRUMBLE

ENOUGH TO GIVE WHAT IS MOST

DEAR. YOUR EARTH.

I was born connected to my mother. With firm and tender intention, she diverted the rivers and streams in her body to form my body. And my body remembers.

It remembers my mother's singing in the rivers and streams, *ra-lala-la . . . ra-lala-lay*. It remembers how she walked in a good quick step and how she rested with warm hands splayed across her body and mine. At night while my mother slept next to my father, I floated in a dream at the end of a long tether. Gently the waters lifted, gently lowered.

One day I was pulled kicking and screaming from the body of my mother. The long swooping cord connecting us was cut.

No matter. The deed was done. I am flesh of my mother's flesh, bone of my mother's bone, made according to the design that she and my father planned together.

She fashioned my large dark eyes. He made the deep and dreaming space behind my eyes. She took her hands and shaped my lips, and my wide bright smile. My father's hand made my tongue and laid stories there, and clear, true singing. When he was finished, my mother made the tip of my tongue, for wit and plain speaking. Then she put a little wave in my hair to remind her of the sea at Bristol where she was born. And my father painted just the slightest trace of red in the wave to remind him of his red-haired mother who died when he was born.

And so it was that my father and mother made me according to the design that they worked out together. But I am earth of my mother's earth, bone of my mother's bone. I was born connected.

I was connected before I was born. Before my mother and father were born, and their mothers and fathers, before the earth was born and time, long, long before then I was connected to the spirit of God so that there never was a time when I did not exist. And my spirit remembers the spirit of God.

It remembers how God diverted deep rivers and endless streams into my spirit. It remembers the humming of God in the rivers and streams and how the waves rose and curled in the humming. My spirit remembers the warm breath of God over the waters and the name of God that rose and fell in the warm breath.

One day the spirit of God made me a tongue and put the name of God that is compassion there. In my eyes the spirit of God put darkness and light, evening and morning, birds, fish, every kind of wild beast and tame, the very image of God. And my eyes remember.

So do my ears. Every time I hear the words, "Do this and remember me," my spirit remembers the supper, the kiss in the garden, and long before when the garden was created, and long, long before that. My spirit remembers floating in the spirit of God and how I was connected long before I was born.

Some day God who put the breath in me will call the breath back. On that day my body will lie down in the earth next to the body of my mother. There will be two times carved in stone over me — the time when I began and the time when I ended.

Do not believe it. There never was a time when I did not exist.

Sometimes I feel the cord coming out of my center connecting me to God. Then I remember how I always was connected to God and how I always will be. Mostly, I remember how I cannot live without God.

LuraMedia Publications

BANKSON, MARJORY ZOET
Braided Streams: *Esther and a Woman's Way of Growing*
Seasons of Friendship: *Naomi and Ruth as a Pattern*

BOHLER, CAROLYN STAHL
Prayer on Wings: *A Search for Authentic Prayer*

BOZARTH, ALLA RENEE
Womanpriest: *A Personal Odyssey (Rev. Ed.)*

GEIGER, LURA JANE
Astonish Me, Yahweh Leader's Guide

and **PATRICIA BACKMAN**
Braided Streams Leader's Guide

and **SUSAN TOBIAS**
Seasons of Friendship Leader's Guide

and **SANDY LANDSTEDT, MARY GECKELER, PEGGIE OURY**
Astonish Me, Yahweh!: *A Bible Workbook-Journal*

JEVNE, RONNA FAY
It All Begins With Hope: *Patients, Caretakers, and the Bereaved Speak Out*

and **ALEXANDER LEVITAN**
No Time for Nonsense: *Getting Well Against the Odds*

KEIFFER, ANN
Gift of the Dark Angel: *A Woman's Journey through Depression toward Wholeness*

LODER, TED
Eavesdropping on the Echoes: *Voices from the Old Testament*
Guerrillas of Grace: *Prayers for the Battle*
No One But Us: *Personal Reflections on Public Sanctuary*
Tracks in the Straw: *Tales Spun from the Manger*
Wrestling the Light: *Ache and Awe in the Human-Divine Struggle*

LUCIANI, JOSEPH
Healing Your Habits: *Introducing Directed Imagination*

MCMAKIN, JACQUELINE
with **SONYA DYER**
Working from the Heart: *For Those Who Search for Meaning and Satisfaction in Their Work*

MEYER, RICHARD C.
One Anothering: *Biblical Building Blocks for Small Groups*

MILLETT, CRAIG
In God's Image: *Archetypes of Women in Scripture*

O'CONNOR, ELIZABETH
Search for Silence *(Revised Edition)*

RAFFA, JEAN BENEDICT
The Bridge to Wholeness: *A Feminine Alternative to the Hero Myth*

SAURO, JOAN
Whole Earth Meditation: *Ecology for the Spirit*

SCHAPER, DONNA
A Book of Common Power: *Narratives Against the Current*
Stripping Down: *The Art of Spiritual Restoration*

WEEMS, RENITA J.
Just a Sister Away: *A Womanist Vision of Women's Relationships in the Bible*

The Women's Series

BORTON, JOAN
Drawing from the Women's Well: *Reflections from the Life Passage of Menopause*

CARTLEDGE-HAYES, MARY
To Love Delilah: *Claiming the Women of the Bible*

DAHL, JUDY
River of Promise: *Two Women's Story of Love and Adoption*

DUERK, JUDITH
Circle of Stones: *Woman's Journey to Herself*

RUPP, JOYCE
The Star in My Heart: *Experiencing Sophia, Inner Wisdom*

SCHAPER, DONNA
Superwoman Turns 40: *The Story of One Woman's Intentions to Grow Up*

LuraMedia, Inc. , 7060 Miramar Rd., Suite 104, San Diego, CA 92121
Books for Healing and Hope, Balance and Justice.